BODY ART

ALISON HAWES

Badger Publishing Limited
Oldmedow Road,
Hardwick Industrial Estate,
King's Lynn PE30 4JJ
Telephone: 01438 791037
www.badgerlearning.co.uk

2 4 6 8 10 9 7 5 3

Body Art ISBN 978-1-78147-819-6

Publisher: Susan Ross
Senior Editor: Danny Pearson
Publishing Assistant: Claire Morgan
Designer: Fiona Grant
Series Consultant: Dee Reid

Photos: Cover Image: GS/Gallery Stock
Page 4: Design Pics Inc/REX
Page 5: Richard Gardner/REX
Page 7: Moviestore Collection/REX
Page 8: © Allen Russell/Alamy
Page 10: Eye Ubiquitous/REX
Page 12: Design Pics Inc/REX
Page 13: © zysman/iStock
Page 14: Tim Graham/Robert Harding/REX
Page 15: © Travelscape Images/Alamy
Page 16: Tumpa Mondal/REX
Page 17: Image Broker/REX
Page 18: © Prisma Bildagentur AG/Alamy
Page 19: © Richard Ellis/Alamy
Page 20: Andre Camara/REX
Page 21: Neil Hall/REX
Page 22: Back Page Images/REX
Page 23: Eric Charles/PYMCA/REX
Page 24: Jean-Luc Brouard/PYMCA/REX
Page 25: © mediacolor's/Alamy
Page 26: Caiaimage/REX
Page 27: © TAO Images Limited/Alamy
Page 28: Startraks Photo/REX
Page 29: Image Broker/REX
Page 30: Image Broker/REX

Attempts to contact all copyright holders have been made.
If any omitted would care to contact Badger Learning, we will be happy to make appropriate arrangements.

Contents

Vocabulary

Aborigine   festival
ancient   henna
androids   latex
celebrate   symbols
enemies   warriors

1. War paint

For thousands of years, people have painted their faces and bodies in times of war.

They do this:
- to stay hidden
- to frighten their enemies

Blue faces

The ancient Britons painted their faces with blue paint before they went into battle.

The blue paint made them look scary and it frightened their enemies!

The blue colour was made from the leaves of a plant.

WOW! facts

In England, long ago, people painted their faces with white make-up made from lead. Then they found out that the lead was poisonous!

Special meanings

Native American warriors put on war paint before they went into battle. They also used it to show their place in the tribe.

The war paint was made up of different colours and symbols. Each of the colours and symbols had a special meaning.

Colour	Meanings
(dark red circle)	war blood
(black circle)	strength death power
(white circle)	a hero death
(grey circle)	wisdom

Symbol	Meanings
(handprint symbol)	brave, good at hand-to-hand fighting
(zigzag symbol)	speed and power
(double triangle symbol)	war

2. Celebrations

Some people paint their face or body to celebrate a special time in their lives.

They may paint their face or body:
- when they get married
- when they become an adult

Henna hands

Many Hindu and Muslim women have patterns painted on their hands and feet to celebrate getting married.

The patterns are painted with a special paste made with henna powder.

Henna powder is made from the leaves of the henna plant.

To make henna paste

You need:

1. Henna powder
2. Lemon juice
3. Sugar
4. Oil

WOW! facts

Most body paints only last for a day or two but henna can last for two weeks before it fades.

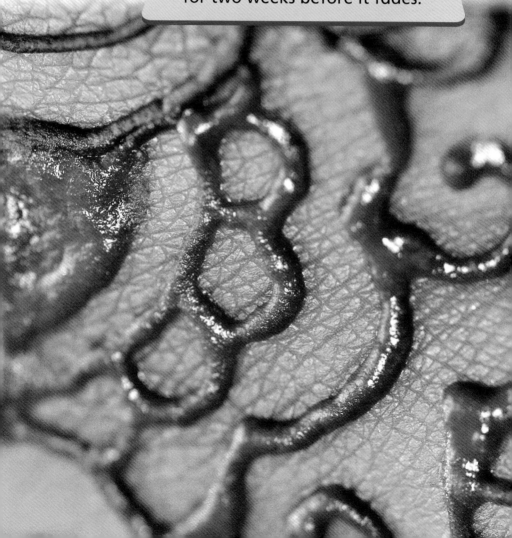

Growing up
In Africa, young Masai men paint their faces white to celebrate becoming an adult.

In Australia, young Aborigine men do the same thing, but they paint their bodies white too.

3. Festivals

Festivals are held all over the world at different times of the year.

At festivals, people often:
- dress up
- paint their faces and bodies

This child is dressed up for a festival in India.
He has been painted blue to look like a Hindu god.

Hindus believe it will bring them good luck if they give
gifts to children dressed up as gods.

Day of the Dead

The Day of the Dead is an important festival in Mexico.

During this festival, people celebrate the lives of their dead relatives.

People dress up as skeletons and paint their faces to look like skulls.

There is music at the festival – and sugar skulls and coffins for sale!

Carnivals and clowns

Every year, a big carnival is held in Brazil in a city called Rio.

People dress up in bright costumes and paint their faces.

Clowns paint their faces in bright colours.

Each clown has his own way of painting his face.

WOW! facts

Did you know that make-up
can have whale vomit, crushed
beetles and animal fat in it?

x

x

Clowns paint their faces in bright colours.

Each clown has his own way of painting his face.

WOW! facts

Did you know that make-up
can have whale vomit, crushed
beetles and animal fat in it?

4. IDENTITY

Some people use body art to show:
- which team they support
- which group they belong to

At big sports events, some fans use body art to show which team they want to win.

They paint their faces in their team's colours or to look like the flag of their country.

Goths and punks

Some people choose to belong to a group that likes the same things and likes to look a certain way.

Goths

Some goths paint their faces white. They often dye their hair black and wear black lipstick. They usually wear black clothes.

Punks

Punks like spiky hair. They dye their hair bright colours. They often wear lots of eyeliner and bright lipstick. They wear ripped clothes.

Nuba

The Nuba people of Africa like to use body art. Each colour is used by a different age group.

Age group	Colours they can use
Young boys	red, white
Older boys	red, white, yellow
Men	red, white, yellow, black

5. Make-up

For thousands of years, people have used make-up to change the way they look.

In ancient times, both men and woman wore make-up. Today, make-up is mostly worn by women.

WOW! facts

In ancient Egypt, men wore eye shadow and eyeliner.

Plays and films

Stage actors sometimes do their own make-up.

Special make-up artists do the make-up for film actors.

In ancient Greece, actors wore masks if they wanted to look different. Now, make-up is used to make an actor look:

- older
- younger
- tired
- ill
- or even dead!

Special effects

Make-up artists are very clever at creating special effects.

They use moulds, latex and paint to change how someone looks.

They can turn an actor into an alien.

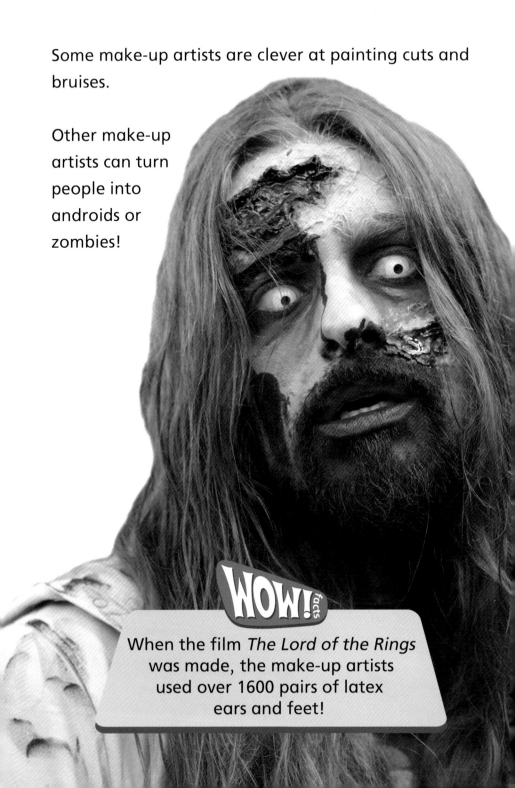

Some make-up artists are clever at painting cuts and bruises.

Other make-up artists can turn people into androids or zombies!

WOW! facts

When the film *The Lord of the Rings* was made, the make-up artists used over 1600 pairs of latex ears and feet!

Questions

What was the blue paint made from that ancient Britons wore? *(page 6)*

What did a painted hand symbol mean on a Native American? *(page 9)*

What is needed to make henna paste? *(page 13)*

How do people celebrate the Day of the Dead in Mexico? *(page 19)*

Where in Brazil does a large carnival take place each year? *(page 20)*

Index